P9-CAM-532

DEVOTIONS
FOR
INSOMNIACS

Books in This Series

By Cecil B. Murphey
　　Devotions for Joggers
　　Devotions for Calorie Counters
　　Devotions for Lovers
　　Devotions for Travelers
　　Devotions for Worriers

By Phillip Barnhart
　　Devotions for Insomniacs

DEVOTIONS
FOR
INSOMNIACS

Phillip Barnhart

SPIRE ✞ BOOKS
Fleming H. Revell Company
Old Tappan, New Jersey

Unless otherwise identified, Scripture quotations are from the Revised Standard Version of the Bible, copyrighted 1946, 1952, © 1971 and 1973.

Scripture quotation identified KJV is from the King James Version of the Bible.

Scripture quotations identified TEV are from the *Good News Bible*—Old Testament: Copyright © American Bible Society 1976: New Testament: Copyright © American Bible Society 1966, 1971, 1976.

Scripture quotation identified TLB is taken from The Living Bible, copyright © 1971 by Tyndale House Publishers, Wheaton, IL. Used by permission.

Scripture quotations identified WEYMOUTH are from WEYMOUTH'S NEW TESTAMENT IN MODERN SPEECH by Richard Francis Weymouth. Published by special arrangement with James Clarke & Company, Ltd., and reprinted by permission of Harper & Row, Publishers, Inc.

Scripture quotation identified JERUSALEM is from The Jerusalem Bible, © 1966 by Darton, Longman & Todd, Ltd. and Doubleday and Company, Inc. Used by permission of the publishers.

Scripture quotation identified NEB is from The New English Bible. © The Delegates of the Oxford University Press and the Syndics of the Cambridge University Press 1961 and 1970. Reprinted by permission.

DEVOTIONS
FOR
INSOMNIACS

Why Don't I Sleep?

> The very night when Herod was about to bring
> him out, Peter was sleeping between two sol-
> diers, bound with two chains.
>
> Acts 12:6

Week 1, Day 1

I tossed and turned, adjusted the pillow for the twen-
tieth time, and checked the clock for the fourth time.
Sleep, an elusive bedfellow, would not come. Finally I
got up again to pace the floor for half an hour.

Back into bed, I tried once more to get to sleep. But
trying to sleep is a self-defeating exercise.

My experience contrasted with Peter in prison.
Chained between two burly soldiers, expecting execu-
tion the next morning, and locked in a dark dungeon, he
slept like a baby.

When I think of Peter asleep in spite of such incredi-
ble circumstances, I wish I were like him.

Many of us long for a rest that won't come. We get out
of bed, leave a wife or husband who's sound asleep, and
go down the hall past the rooms of our snoring children.

If they can sleep, why can't I? we ask ourselves.

Why? We come up with many reasons:

1. Too much left unaccomplished today.
2. I'm not ready for tomorrow's big day.
3. I hurt someone and can't get it out of my mind.
4. The late-night bologna sandwich won't digest.
5. That television program still has me in its clutches.

Now we ask another question: which of these intrusions could I have avoided with little or no trouble?

I used to read the newspaper late at night. I'd go to bed and take the world's problems with me. The starving children, political deceit in high places, wars around the globe kept me awake. Still I wondered why I couldn't sleep. One night, finally asleep, I had a nightmare. In the nightmare a military tank plodded behind me, spitting out its orange and charcoal fire as the flames lapped at my feet. Waking, I got out of bed and kicked over a glass of milk I'd left on the floor. Turning on the light so I could clean up the mess, I saw the newspaper I'd been reading: "War Breaks Out Again in Northern Ireland" and under the heading, a picture of a tank.

I can't take the world's problems to bed with me and sleep. So now I avoid them. That's one reason for sleeplessness I can do something about.

As we think of the reasons we can't sleep we can come up with a method for dealing with most of them. For example:

1. I won't eat bologna sandwiches before I go to bed.
2. If I've hurt anybody, I'll set it right that day.
3. I'll watch only light television programs late at night.

What we know by insight we can change by foresight.

O God, you enabled Simon Peter to sleep even when he couldn't change the circumstances. Help me change what I can and accept what I can't. Amen.

Finding an Image

The Lord is my shepherd, I shall not want.

Psalms 23:1

Week 1, Day 2

I lay awake at night, work done for the day, but still treading the mill. My daughter's hearing aid broke, and it must be repaired tomorrow; she can hardly hear a word without it. There's no repair shop in the whole county. Where will I go? Will they be able to fix it? These questions intruded on my sleep.

I asked several people to share with me their intrusions. Fred said it was his temper tantrum that day. Julie, her unwillingness to keep the house straightened up. Harriet had lost a pair of earrings her mother had given her.

Insomniacs can't turn their minds off. The present day or the next day keeps crowding in. Think of the last time you couldn't get to sleep. What was the unwelcome intruder? How do we deal with these situations? Try more willpower? Tell ourselves it's silly? Take a sleeping pill? Walk the floor?

I've tried many ways to shut off my mind, most of them unsuccessful. One night, still up at 3:00 A.M., I looked out the window. I saw only darkness, but I knew there was a grassy and peaceful meadow behind the house. I couldn't see it, but with my imagination I envi-

Devotions for Insomniacs

sioned the meadow and pictured myself lying in the middle of it without a care in the world. Soon a peace came, and my eyelids grew heavy. I relaxed in a nearby overstuffed chair and fell asleep.

I'd found a substitute for the intruders upon my sleep. Since then, I've compiled a list of peaceful, tranquil scenes and focus on them when insomnia works over-time.

Yet no image has helped me more than the first three verses of Psalm 23.

Verse 1: If God really is my Shepherd and meets my needs, what could I possibly want enough to keep me awake?

Verse 2: God enables me to lie down and sleep. God wills for me to rest. To rest in green pastures (green is the color of life and wholeness) presents the image of calm and ease.

Verse 3: God leads me beside still waters, no turbu-lence, and he does the leading. I don't have to map out the course. He leads me in paths of righteousness and if I am rightly related to God, I don't need to fret into the wee hours of the morning. He does it all for his name's sake. It is to his glory and honor that I sleep.

Many nights now God enables me to lie down in green pastures, leads me beside still waters and down paths of righteousness. Occasionally, I don't let him have his way; but the more I practice this kind of imag-ing, the easier it becomes to fall asleep.

Dear loving Shepherd, help me see the images of peace and rest you have placed all around me. Amen.

Setting Things Straight

"Be at peace with one another."

Mark 9:50

Week 1, Day 3

Tony keeps a resolution he made four years ago. If humanly possible, he never goes to bed without attempting a reconciliation with anyone he's offended that day. And Tony's gotten to sleep more quickly the last four years than any other period of his life.

He says, "I realized the unfinished business of my relationships kept me awake—a thoughtless word I'd spoken, a careless slight of one dear to me. A friend directed me to Matthew 5:23, 24. I read it nine times before God gave me the power to commit its promise to my life. At the seventh reading, I changed the Scripture to fit me. I put in the words, 'If I have offended anyone this day.' Two days later I insulted one of my seventh grade students; I called her stupid! Ten o'clock that night I was getting ready for bed when I remembered Matthew 5 and my student at the same time. It was a most difficult thing to do, but I phoned Kara, apologized, and said I really appreciated her. I went to bed with the day's business finished and slept like a baby. Since then, I try to mend broken relationships one day at a time. And God's given me a bonus: I don't have as many to mend because

I'm more careful about what I say and do."

Saint Paul, in Romans 12:18, says, "If possible, so far as it depends upon you, live peaceably with all." It's not always possible to live peaceably with everyone, but at the end of each day we can assess our behavior and set right what went wrong.

But what if someone won't accept my apology? I've never had that happen. The human spirit is kinder than we think, and most people receive apologies graciously. In fact, most to whom I apologize tell me I didn't need to at all; they'd already forgiven me. But I did need to—if not for them, certainly for me, for my peace and sleep.

I was terribly unfair to my daughter Lisa, and had already lost one night's sleep over it. The next day I said, "Honey, Daddy didn't treat you right and I'm sorry."

"That's okay, Daddy," she replied, "it ain't no big thing." It was a big thing to me, but once I set it straight it was nothing at all.

Remember that Saint Paul said, "so far as it depends upon you." It does depend on us, doesn't it?

Lord Jesus, who taught and lived forgiveness, give me the courage to ask for it when I need it. Amen.

Nature Speaks

> When I look at thy heavens, the work of thy
> fingers, the moon and stars which thou hast
> established. . . .
>
> Psalms 8:3

Week 1, Day 4

I'm a lucky fellow. I can walk across the street to one
of the most beautiful lakes in the world, Geneva Lake in
southern Wisconsin.

Often at night, when I can't sleep, I do. It's possible to
walk all the way around the lake's twenty-four-mile
shoreline, but a mile is usually enough to consider God's
handiwork and get in tune with him.

God writes his name on the garments of nature. When
I read it there, I'm more peaceful and restful. If God can
create that gorgeous lake or that glamorous sunset,
surely he can take care of me through the night. If he
can take care of me through the night, shouldn't I let
him?

God's revelation through nature can be a sleeping pill
᠁ us. Getting in touch with the beauty of the earth is a
tra᠁ We᠁lizer with only the best side effects.

or at the᠁is when we're on vacation in the mountains
setting. Bu᠁e or when we're on a retreat in a rustic
where we are, ᠁do it whenever we need to, right
Think of a par᠁᠁ live in an asphalt jungle.
᠁ of woods or a vacant hill-

side within a mile of where you live. Can you go there when you can't sleep? Will you?

Harvey goes out in his backyard. Two weeping willows hang their delicate leaves there. Harvey looks at them for a while, then climbs a few feet up into one and sits there secluded and protected. In his seclusion he feels secure, at one with the God of the willow trees.

Rachel walks four blocks to the local playground, sits in one of the swings, gazes at the pond, and listens to the movement of the mallards. Soon she is calm and ready for bed.

Jimmy jogs a mile to the high-school football field. Nobody's there but him. He lies down on the twenty-yard line and looks up at the sky. Soon the peacefulness of the sky calms him, and he's ready to go home.

Where can you go? The next time you can't sleep, pick a place and make the effort to get there. There, meditate on the grandeur of God—our God who makes the sunset, causes the birds to sing, erects a hill and sets it against the sky. "O Lord, our Lord, how majestic is thy name in all the earth!" (Psalms 8:9).

God of heaven and earth, thank you for writing your name on the garments of nature where I can see it and be blessed by it. Amen.

Dreams

> But God came to Laban the Aramean in a
> dream by night.
>
> Genesis 31:24

Week 1, Day 5

I've had the same dream several times during the last seven years. In the dream I go back to the church I previously pastored, a once declining church in a black community. Our assignment, in 1967, was to save that church and minister to the neighborhood. God led us in a great ministry, but when I left the church in 1975, some people thought the church would decline once again. I worried that it would; that worry kept me awake many nights. In my dream, when I'm transported back, I hardly recognize the building. It's been renovated, added on to, and sparkles. When I enter the building, it's filled with activity: Bible classes, tutorial programs, counseling groups. I see several of my former parishioners, and guess what? They're kind and loving, but they don't recognize me.

God uses that dream to speak to me. "You're not indispensable," he says. "Trust me to continue my work."

In his book *Dreams: A Way to Listen to God*, Morton Kelsey says, "Every person today can experience the power of God through the dream if he or she is really open to this possibility." But most of us shut out supernatural revelation that comes to us through the world of dreams. We determine that spiritual reality is known only through reason, our senses, and Scripture.

Nothing could be further from the biblical witness. In a dream Jacob saw God standing above a ladder, promising to be his companion. Joseph kept the world from starving by listening to his dreams. Another Joseph learned of the Messiah's coming through a dream, and that Messiah was protected by the wise men who paid attention to their dreams.

My friend John says he can hardly wait to get to sleep to see what God will say to him through his dreams. John keeps a pad and pencil near his bed, has learned to wake himself up from his dreams, records every detail, and asks God to help him understand any message there is. I'm not that far along; I don't want to conclude God speaks when it's just the pizza I ate. But I am open to the voice of God in my dreams.

Here's another dream I had: I'm playing in a championship basketball game. There's one second left on the time clock, and the score is tied as I let loose a thirty-five-foot shot. The final whistle blows with the ball in midair; the ball shoots down toward the basket, zips through the net, and the crowd roars. God and I worked on that dream a long time before I understood its meaning. I'd always wanted to be a super basketball player, never was, and settled in as an avid fan. God told me, through my dream, to enjoy watching others score the winning points in basketball, but that I had and would score the winning points in other areas of life.

The lesson in all this for insomniacs is: don't be afraid

to fall asleep at night. God may have a message for you. He may answer a prayer you've made during the day, clarify a confusing issue, interpret a circumstance you can't fathom.

O God, who spoke to Abraham and others through dreams, speak to me. Amen.

One Part at a Time

Even in the night his mind does not rest.
                                  Ecclesiastes 2:23

Week 1, Day 6

Gene said, "I can't get to sleep and you gotta help me."

Who am I to help you? I thought. How many nights I pace the floor and wear out the rug. Struggling to give an answer to Gene, I remembered a technique I had read about but never tried.

The article suggested relaxing the body, one part at a time, until the whole body is limp. I shared my newly remembered insight with Gene and decided I'd try it myself the next time sleep wouldn't come. Two nights later I lay in bed, my mind going ninety miles an hour. How will I squeeze in all those appointments tomorrow? I haven't spent a whole day with my family in months. Out of desperation I tried the relaxation technique. I worked first on my right arm as it hung over the bed, beginning with the fingers, one at a time, and moving to the wrist, forearm, and elbow. By the time I got to my shoulder I was still dubious and yet hopeful. The neck was next, where most of my tension lives; then I relaxed my face muscles. By the time I got to my eyes they were heavy, and I don't remember anything else.

I told Georgette about my newfound gimmick, and she said she'd been doing that for years. She shared with me a variation; she does it in the bathtub up to her neck in warm soapy water. Mickey does it, flat on the floor, after his five-mile run. Then he crawls into bed. Sonja relaxes her body, one part at a time, while on her knees praying. After she's praised, petitioned, and interceded she relaxes her body, asking God's help. Lifting her hands in the air, she thinks about God's peace coming first into her fingertips, then down through her arms, and so forth, until no part of her body is left untouched.

This technique controls our bodies one part at a time and makes relaxation something we can handle. It also symbolizes that we give our bodies to God and trust him to watch over them during the night.

Holy Spirit, visit my body and fill it with your controlling presence. Amen.

Not Without the Lord

> I will not give sleep to my eyes or slumber to
> my eyelids, until I find a place for the Lord.
> Psalms 132:4, 5

Week 1, Day 7

I've been sleeping better recently. I wondered why, so I asked my best friend. He questioned me about my home life; had any changes taken place? About my work; any recent super successes? I answered no to both questions. "How is your spiritual journey?" he asked.

"What do you mean?" I replied.

"Do you feel close to God? Taking more time to pray? Feeling new power in your life?"

Yes, that's it, I thought. I have made strides in my spiritual development the last few weeks. I feel God's presence most of the time. And, yes, I am sleeping better.

For me, resting at night corresponds to resting in God. I think of the psalmist's words: "I will not give sleep to my eyes or slumber to my eyelids, until I find a place for the Lord." I take the psalmist's statement in two senses:

1. I will not attempt to sleep until I've invited God into my life. I'll be audacious; after all, Jesus did say, "Ask and you will receive."

   2. I cannot sleep until I give God entry into my
      life. It's impossible, and I won't even try it.

When someone asked John Wesley how he'd spend
his time if he knew he only had twenty-four hours to
live, he replied, "Just as I intend to spend it now. I'd
preach this evening at Gloucester and again in the
morning. Then I'd ride to friend Martin's house who ex-
pects to entertain me. I'd pray with the family as usual,
go to bed at ten o'clock, commend my soul to God, lie
down to rest, and wake up in Glory."

God had a dwelling place in the life of John Wesley, a
fact he reminded himself of and affirmed each night before he went to sleep. If he felt out of sorts with God that
day, he set it straight before he turned out the light.

Our commitment to God should never be any older
than twenty-four hours. A good time to renew that commitment is at night in bed. Think on these nighttime
prayers, select the appropriate one each night for a
week, and pray it:

   1. O God, it's been a good day. I felt your pres-
      ence, and I praise you for it. Amen.
   2. O God, you and I started off the day together,
      but somehow I lost sight of you. Return to me
      now. Amen.
   3. O God, this day was all mine and none of
      yours. Forgive me, speak your love to me, be
      with me during the night and the first thing to-
      morrow morning. Amen.

Praying specifically for divine presence focuses on God, establishes a prayer habit, becomes a spiritual inventory, trusts God to be with us, and stretches our souls on the spiritual journey.

O God, thank you that every day you walk with me whether I acknowledge it or not. Amen.

Good and Tired

Sweet is the sleep of a laborer.
                                        Ecclesiastes 5:12

Week 2, Day 1

I worked summers at a steel mill, earning money for college. I worked hard, especially when I shoveled out ore the crane missed in the bottom of the railroad cars. The days I shoveled out ore, those nights I slept like a baby.

Conrad shared his sleeplessness in a small group discussion. Others joined in, relating similar problems. But Tom said nothing. After the meeting Conrad asked, "Tom, don't you have trouble sleeping?"

"Not for years. I'm so exhausted after the middle shift at the plant that I'm almost asleep before I get in bed."

Not all of us have that kind of job. But there are things we can do to tire ourselves out so we can sleep better.

Harmon saves his jogging until late evening. It's cooler then, his neighborhood streets are empty, and the four miles unwind him from the day's pressures. Upon request of his friend Paul, a medical doctor, Harmon keeps a record of his running and his sleeping habits. There's a direct correlation between the degree of physical exhaustion and the time it takes Harmon to get to sleep.

June enrolled in an aerobic-dance class. Aware of Harmon's studies, she chose the evening session. After an hour and a half of demanding routines, her body is so exhausted she thinks of nothing but meeting its needs. Her mind has no interest in going over the day's events.

Evening exercise not only exhausts our bodies but, more important, it occupies our minds. It centers us on one thing and shuts out all that today brought and tomorrow might bring. Exhausting exercise closes doors that are best opened again only after a good night's sleep.

How can we prepare for sleep through physical activity? Jog, run, or walk. Take an exercise class. Work out at the gym. Spend time in the workshop. Play ball with the children. Join a softball or basketball league for adults. Do calisthenics at home, or home cleaning-up projects we've put off.

Bob is a giant of a man, six feet seven inches, two hundred ninety pounds. That's a lot of body to tire out, but Bob believes he has to shut down his body before he can shut off his mind and get to sleep. He built a weight bench in his basement, and each night he works out. Bob also worships on the weight bench. Every time he lifts the bar he says the Jesus prayer: "Lord Jesus, have mercy on me." Bob says, "When I'm anxious, I work. As I work, I worship."

O God, I'll worship as I work and rejoice as I sleep. Amen.

A Case for the Closet

"But thou, when thou prayest, enter into thy
closet."

Matthew 6:6 KJV

Week 2, Day 2

Johnny Carson was in rare form with his political
quips and Jack Benny impressions. I laughed bois-
terously, watched the finale, and turned off the television. Checking the next day's calendar, I set the clock
and switched on the radio to WMAQ Chicago. Conway
Twitty sang of "bridges that won't burn," and Dolly
Parton lamented working "nine to five," and I lay
awake.

Unlike other nights, I knew the problem. Having just
finished a course in meditation techniques, I knew I had
not entered my prayer closet. I had kept the world's
noise at my bedside, creating no separation of the day's
frenzy and the night's potential peace.

As I have read in Richard J. Foster's *Celebration of
Discipline,* "In contemporary society our adversary
majors in three things: noise, hurry, and crowds. If he
can keep us engaged in 'muchness' and 'manyness,' he
will rest satisfied. Psychiatrist C. G. Jung once re-
marked, 'Hurry is not of the Devil, it *is* the Devil.' "

Aware of what I could do to wind down the day and
rest on God's heart pillows, I did it. I looked across the

room at my clothes closet, thought of getting in it, knew there was no space, and turned on my imagination.

I envisioned myself in an empty closet, door closed, on my knees, alone with my Lord. I held in my mind a picture of Jesus that hangs in my study. In the picture he's virile, alive, able. I imagined Jesus knelt beside me in the closet, his face before me, his eyes on my eyes. He said nothing, just looked and smiled. The smile was loving and lingering. It said I'm special to him.

Then I envisioned Jesus kneeling by my side, holding my hand, and facing with me whatever I faced the next day: my job, my family, my allies and adversaries. This time he spoke, no long discourses or sermons, just phrases of assurance: "I'll be with you." "We'll do it together." "You can count on me." Then Jesus asked me to lie down on the floor with him and look up. Some words I'd read came to me: "When the outlook is bad, try the uplook." Jesus said, "Look beyond the ceiling and see the sky, the sky and our Father who watches us as we look for him." The next thing I remember is the 6:00 A.M. radio alarm and the popular song, "Footprints in the Sand." In the song, a man asks Jesus why, when times were tough, there was only one set of footprints in the sand. "Didn't you promise always to walk with me?" Jesus replies, "My son, when you see only one set of footprints in the sand, I carried you." Jesus, who knelt with me in imagination's closet, carried me peacefully through the night.

Lord Jesus, it's you and me now face to face. Thank you for your look of love. Amen.

Breathing in God

Let everything that breathes praise the Lord!
Psalms 150:6

Week 2, Day 3

Breath is a meaningful symbol to me. God breathed life into me when I was born. I use breath to continue life in this world. I get out of breath trying to do the things I feel I must do. I have breath to praise God for the creation, maintenance, and activity of life.

Thinking of the gift of breath, a few years ago I began using breathing exercises as I prepared to sleep.

The basic one I use and build on: I inhale and exhale to a count of two. One—inhale, two—exhale. I don't count higher than two or I'll concentrate too much on the numbers. I feel the place in my body, usually the abdomen, where the breathing pulls at me. I focus on that spot and ask God to begin there to relax me.

Sometimes I vary this exercise: On the inhale I say "Je-" and on the exhale I say "-sus." "Je-sus." "Je-sus." I think of the Lord whose name I call.

Another variation: I think of some characteristics of my life I want to get rid of, some characteristics I'd like to bring into my life. On the inhale I concentrate on the qualities I want; on the exhale, the qualities I don't want. For instance: Inhale peace—exhale anxiety. Inhale confidence—exhale insecurity. Frequently I focus on habits I want to get rid of and those I desire as part of my life.

Yet another way I use breathing as preparation for sleep: I breathe in and out as rapidly as I can, turn my breathing into panting. I wear myself out. Exhausted, I repeat Psalms 150:6 with the breath I have left, "Let everything that breathes praise the Lord! Praise the Lord!"

O God, thank you for reasons to praise you and resources to praise you with. Amen.

Dwell on the Good

O give thanks to the Lord, for he is good, for
his steadfast love endures for ever.

Psalms 136:1

Week 2, Day 4

Martha believed nothing good ever happened to her;
she lay awake at night fretting over her bad luck. The
failures and defeats she'd suffered became a list she went
over again and again: a broken marriage, a rebellious
son, an unfulfilling job. I invited Martha to look at the
good in her life. She remembered her faithful Sunday
school children, parents who think she's beautiful and
intelligent, a daughter who is her best friend. The list's
length surprised Martha as we talked about each ac-
complishment. I asked her to write down all the good
things, keep them on her nightstand, and make them a
part of her preparation for sleep.

"Read Psalms 136," I said. "Look at your list and affirm how God's steadfast love endures in your life. Notice in the psalm that after every praise for a specific act
of God, there is the affirmation, 'for his steadfast love
endures for ever.' For two weeks I want you to read your
list out loud item by item, and after each one add the
words, 'for his steadfast love endures for ever.' " After
two weeks Martha reported an improved self-image, a

greater awareness of God's love, and an easier time getting to sleep.

To deny the good in our lives is just as foolish as to deny the bad. We have been too long in the practice of studying sickness and need to study the wholeness in us. Reflect on the good fortune we have.

Here are a few statements we insomniacs can read if we have trouble sleeping:

1. I am made in the image of God.
2. God doesn't make junk.
3. God doesn't sponsor flops.
4. I am an unrepeatable miracle of God.
5. I am a special child of God.
6. In God's eyes, I am *somebody!*

Let's also give thought to these: Today

1. Someone leaned on me or asked for my help.
2. I did my job well.
3. My husband/wife told me how much I mean to him/her.
4. My child put his/her arms around me.
5. Someone at the church made me feel I belong.
6. The supermarket clerk said my smile made her day.

These may not fit every person, but we need to identify the good in our lives and give ourselves the strokes we deserve. We need to think of the God who makes us special and causes good things to happen to us and through us. The God who walks with us during the day watches over us through the night and is there to greet us in the morning. His steadfast love endures forever!

O God, thank you for believing in me enough to get me here, stay with me, and lead me on. Amen.

Leave Tomorrow Alone

"Therefore do not be anxious about tomorrow."

Matthew 6:34

Week 2, Day 5

I've learned to handle yesterday and today fairly well.
Tomorrow keeps me awake: the appointments, the programs to plan, the phone calls to make. I go to bed
dwelling on tomorrow, toss and turn, finally fall asleep
from exhaustion, and wake up early with the agenda
clicking away in my mind.

But recently I've gotten some help from a self-indict-
ment. How foolish all that is. Reflecting on the foolish-
ness I came up with some questions.

1. What can I do here in bed about tomorrow?
2. Can I keep tomorrow's appointments here in
   bed?
3. Can I make my phone calls at 3:00 in the morning?
4. Can I plan the programs tomorrow if I stay
   awake worrying about them tonight?

The conclusion: I can't do a thing about tomorrow, at
least not tonight.

Marvin doesn't worry about what *will* happen tomorrow; he worries about what *might* happen. I do, too. And

I bet you do. Marvin and I talked, and we asked ourselves these questions:

1. What do we worry about that doesn't happen?
2. Or couldn't happen?
3. Or if it happened, wouldn't amount to much of
   anything?

Then we put a percentage on each category. In almost
all cases the accumulated totals came out to nearly 100.
We decided the rest we'd leave in the hands of God or
accept as healthy surprises.

Really, what can we do about tomorrow tonight? How
much sleep do we lose fretting about the impossible and
the improbable?

Margie found a way to deal with anxiety about tomorrow. She read C. S. Lewis: "Anxiety is a sin we need
to ask God to forgive." She shared the quote with me,
and I asked her what it meant to her. This is what she
said: "God makes promises to take care of me. God
keeps his promises and asks me to trust his promises.
When I don't, I'm disobedient and disobedience is a
sin."

Could it be that when we stay awake worrying about
tomorrow, we deny the ability of God to do what he says
he'll do (take care of us)?

Even if worry is not a sin, it is an unnecessary intruder
upon our sleep. I heard E. Stanley Jones say, "Worry is
advance interest we pay on a debt that never comes
due." Seldom does what we worry about happen or,
when it does, amount to anything like what we thought
it would.

*Lord Jesus, who taught us to trust God in the future, teach
us to live one day at a time with you. Amen.*

Shake Off the Dust

"And if any one will not receive you or listen to your words, shake off the dust from your feet as you leave."

Matthew 10:14

Week 2, Day 6

For some, tomorrow doesn't keep them awake, but yesterday does. Like Ronnie, an insurance agent. For every policy he sells, five people don't buy. At night, when he should be asleep, Ronnie goes over every interview. What didn't I say? Should I have concentrated more on the husband? Did I come on too strong?

I am a minister who wants important things to happen in my congregation. My disappointments go to bed with me. I mull them over until I'm a nervous, wide-awake wreck. I cry out, "O God, help me make it through the night."

God helps me through the night when he challenges me to bury yesterday. When people die, we bury them; when the ambitions and dreams of the past die, we should bury them also.

No Scripture has helped me as much with my yesterdays as Matthew 10:14. Jesus wants his disciples to preach salvation to the lost sheep of Israel. He desires that they succeed: heal the sick, raise the dead, cleanse lepers, cast out demons, and make the kingdom of God a present reality. That's quite an assignment. If the disciples fail, will they be able to sleep at night? After all, Jesus is Lord and he's given them orders.

But Jesus is a realist. He knows his men won't hit the ball every time they get up to bat; he makes provisions for defeat. When people turn a deaf ear to you, he says, "shake the dust from your feet, leave them, and get on with the next thing. Don't lay awake at night lamenting what wasn't accomplished."

God doesn't expect us to be perfect or to win every time. The Bible is full of those who failed. Simon Peter denied, Thomas doubted, Mark left Paul and ran home. You and I fail. We fail God, ourselves, others.

But that's yesterday. And yesterdays are "a bucket of ashes," Carl Sandburg said. God does not want us to wallow in yesterday. Today is his gift to us. Let's shake off the dust of past failures and get on with the life we have now.

O God, who accepts my failures better than I do, thank you for understanding who I am. Amen.

No Separation

For I am sure that neither death, nor life . . . nor things present, nor things to come, nor powers, nor height, nor depth, nor anything else in all creation will be able to separate us from the love of God in Christ Jesus our Lord.

Romans 8:38, 39

Week 2, Day 7

As children, our parents taught us the bedtime prayer: "Now I lay me down to sleep. I pray the Lord my soul to keep. If I should die before I wake, I pray the Lord my soul to take." That prayer is criticized because it makes children think they might die in their sleep. I *have* heard several people tell of psychological trauma caused by such a thought, and I agree that it's not a good prayer for children.

However, mature Christians can pray it with meaning. As a child it frightened me, but now it assures me. No matter what happens while I sleep, God takes care of me. He keeps my soul on earth or he takes my soul to heaven. Either way, we are with God. Nothing can separate us from his love.

Jay used to worry he'd die in his sleep. As long as he was awake he felt in control, but when he lay down to sleep he felt helpless. Having a weak heart, he knew many heart attacks occur during the night when the body temperature is at its lowest, and he frequently stayed awake, afraid to even close his eyes. That was before Jay received Jesus as his Lord and claimed the promise of eternal life. Now, just before pulling the covers up, every night he repeats in a triumphant voice, "Nothing can separate *me* from the love of God in Jesus my Lord." Then he pauses and says even more triumphantly, "Not even *death!*"

It's not fatalistic resignation I advocate. I want to live at least twice as long as I've already lived, which will put me near the end of my ninth decade, but I trust God to provide for me no matter what. It's not a disdain for this world I advocate. I love my life, my friends and family, my work; but I know I'll be happy in heaven also.

God's love for us continues throughout eternity. It is both timely and timeless. When we believe this, we can sleep, assured God will live with us no matter what the location of our residence.

Now I lay me down to sleep; the Lord my soul will keep. If I die before I wake, the Lord my soul will take. Amen.

Before We Go to Sleep

Do not let the sun go down on your anger.
Ephesians 4:26

Week 3, Day 1

My friend Bill walks closely with Jesus and possesses a peace I've seen in few people. Certain he never experiences insomnia, I said, "Bill, you don't ever have trouble getting to sleep, do you?"

He replied, "Only once in my life, and that was shortly after Stephen's death." (Bill's son, Stephen, was accidentally killed when twelve years old.)

"What was involved in that sleeplessness was due to my unresolved anger that the doctors refused to take Stephen's body off the respirator and my difficulty in forgiving them for their insanity. In that brief period when I did have trouble sleeping, I learned the two things that would keep me from healthy sleep: anger and bitterness. These two cancers are gone from my life, long gone, and I sleep very well, as I always have except for that difficult period."

Bill learned what we all should learn: Anger keeps us awake. Bill saw the problem and did what he does with all problems; he asked the Lord to help him solve it.

When in his pre-teens, Joey fought every boy on the block. He'd scratch, claw, and bite at a moment's notice.

One day his dad pulled him off a playmate whom he was ferociously beating. Dad carried Joey into the house, put him down hard on the bed, and talked to him for forty-five minutes. What he said made all the difference in Joey's life. He told his son how he'd dealt with anger over the years and encouraged him to do the same.

"Don't go to sleep without asking yourself if your temper got out of hand today. Tell God where you went wrong and ask him to give you more control tomorrow. You and God deal with your anger before you call it a day." That was eight years ago; Joey no longer has temper tantrums, and he's a sound sleeper.

Before I knew where it came from, I was aware of this verse from Ephesians, for Mom often said, "Son, don't go to bed angry." We can examine our behavior daily and run an inventory on the day's events. Was I unnecessarily harsh to my husband/wife? Did I growl at my neighbor for no good reason? Or even if I had a good reason, was that what God wanted me to do?

Dealing daily with our anger gives strength to do better and peace to sleep better.

O Lord, forgive me for my anger. Calm my soul, control my tongue, and show me a new way to live tomorrow. Amen.

Open Doors

"Behold, I have set before you an open door,
which no one is able to shut. . . ."

Revelation 3:8

Week 3, Day 2

Bill Cadle was once a hopeless alcoholic and later
directed a home for the healing of alcoholics. He ex-
plained the difference between his former and latter
lives by saying, "I used to wake up and say, 'Good God,
it's morning'; now I wake up and say, 'Good morning,
God.'" I asked Bill what he meant and he replied,
"Now I can't wait to see what doors God will open for
me each day."

Neither can I. Each day God gives me opportunities
to meet and people to love. He throws open doors I
haven't seen, and I stand in rooms I didn't know existed.
Looking forward to such a day, I sleep well. I sleep well
because I want to rest and be ready for what God sends
my way. I know when I wake up, God will be present to
show me where I am to go and what I am to do.

Our tomorrows are filled with God's plans for us. We
can look forward to a spiritual serendipity God designs
for our experience.

Sleep experts say that many people who don't want to
crawl out of bed in the morning are depressed. They

can't face a new day because they think it will be a bad one, full of anguish and defeat. They feel all doors will be closed and the rooms of life they live in will be bare and bleak.

That's not what God has in store for us. He sets before us open doors which no one can shut, if we see them, enter them, and trust God to go with us. Let us stop living only in the basements of our lives when there are rooms upstairs we haven't seen, let alone lived in.

Patricia can't wait to get up in the morning to see what God will do next in her life. Last week she found a little boy lost in a department store, crying his heart out. She soothed him, took him to the store office, had them announce the little boy's plight over the public-address system, and saw him reunited with his parents. The week before, she ran into an old college friend she hadn't seen for twenty years and they spent the evening together. And next week? Patricia joyfully waits to go through the doors God opens for her.

Holy Spirit, I will sleep now, expectantly awaiting what you have for me tomorrow. Amen.

Our Friends

But Peter, standing with the eleven, lifted up
his voice and addressed them.

Acts 2:14

Week 3, Day 3

A few months ago I moved 800 miles away from
where I'd lived for twenty-one years. And I left all my
friends behind. I'm making new ones now, but for several nights I lay awake thinking how bleak tomorrow
would be without my friends, friends who stood with me
and let me stand with them just as Peter and the eleven
faced the world together.

When we think of our friends as we go to bed, we receive a sense of security that helps us relax and rest.
When we mention our friends in our nighttime prayers,
calling their names, thanking God for each of them, we
claim the gift God gives us through them and feel satisfied. Good friends who stick with us remind us of our
great God who provides for all our needs. The harbor of
friendship is the port through which we sail to God
himself. We touch one another and feel the presence of
Jesus, who called his disciples "friends."

Angie doesn't have any close friends. She doesn't re-
late well, turns people off, and spends most of her time
alone. Her father, the best friend she ever had, died re-

cently, and she has even more difficulty sleeping than before.

You know Angie. Maybe that's not the name you know her by, but she's somewhere within your sphere of influence. And she needs you as a friend. There are several like her in my daily world. When I reach out for them, touch them with God's love, they sleep better and so do I.

One friend I left behind stays with me every day. Our friendship is the kind geography can't disturb. He sort of sits on my shoulder now as I tell you about him. He loves me even when he can't understand me, but understands me better than most. He teaches me without condescension and corrects me without condemnation. He affirms me honestly and accepts me sincerely.

Each night before I go to sleep I think of this friend, call his name in prayer, and rest in his arms, arms God has wrapped around me.

Thank you, God, for my friends. Tonight I especially thank you for _____. Amen.

Interruptions

And he went with him. And a great crowd fol-
lowed him and thronged about him. And there
was a woman who had had a flow of blood for
twelve years.

Mark 5:24, 25

Week 3, Day 4

Jairus summons Jesus to heal his daughter and on the
way to Jairus' house, Jesus' journey is interrupted. A
woman, terribly sick for twelve years, needs him. He
honors the interruption and makes her whole again.

We don't do as well with our interruptions, do we? In
bed at night we go over each unscheduled event of the
day, lament the time they took, and stay awake wishing
they hadn't happened.

I emptied my pockets on the nightstand, picked up my
note pad, and scanned the list of things I'd needed to do
that day. Only four of the ten were completed. "But if
there hadn't been those interruptions . . ." I said. In bed
I continued to regret the interruptions, going over each
one in my mind. I stopped as God spoke to me: "Take a
good look at what they were." I did, and my mood
changed. A ten-year-old boy had stopped by my office
on the way to school just to say hello; we talked for
forty-five minutes about the church and Jesus. The hospital called; an accident victim from out of town had no

pastor and I went to be with her husband. I ran into a friend downtown; we went to a restaurant, had a cup of coffee, and talked about his new business venture.

What glorious interruptions! My regret disappeared as I considered the opportunities and blessings the unexpected gave me that day. Instead of staying awake on the note of regret, I went to sleep praising God for scheduling my day for me.

Interruptions are often the best part of the day: people we like to be with, but haven't seen for a while, strangers who are only friends we hadn't met yet; challenges that make us reach back for something extra we didn't know we had.

Let us:

1. Savor the interruptions of today.
2. Praise God for them.
3. Look forward to what tomorrow will bring.
4. Ask God for wisdom to recognize, patience to claim, and freedom to enjoy whatever he sends our way.

Dear Lord, schedule my tomorrow as you desire and let me see your will in all that happens. Amen.

Better Than Today

"But you have kept the good wine until now."
                                          John 2:10

Week 3, Day 5

Ivan says, "I get up in the morning and read the obituary column; when I don't find my name in it, I figure I'll have a pretty good day."

After serious brain surgery and a long recuperation, Ivan considers just to live another day a gift from God. Ivan also believes something else. "How was your day, Ivan?" I asked.

"Better than yesterday, and tomorrow will be better than today." He receives each day as an opportunity to grow. He looks forward to improving his talent and doing his job more efficiently. As he turns in for the night, he anticipates improvement and maturation tomorrow. He's seldom disappointed. For him, insomnia is only a word in the dictionary.

God wants to change us each day. The wine of our lives can get better and better. We can learn tomorrow what we didn't know today, become more emotionally whole, and live in the mansions we dream about tonight.

Jesus turned the plain, pale water into the full red blush of superior wine, the best they'd ever tasted.

What a thought to go to bed on! We don't have to be

tomorrow as we are today. We can know more, grow
more, have more to go on because Jesus takes what is
and works a miracle with it.

When we let him, that is. We choose to either inhibit or
enable our growth. Intentionality furnishes the key. Preparing for sleep is a good time to decide tomorrow will
be greater than today, even if today was special. I used
to give myself a pep talk about tomorrow only when
today was rotten. "It's gotta be better tomorrow;
couldn't be any worse." Since I heard Jesus invite me to
grow, I pray that each day will top the preceding one,
even if it was super. I believe Jesus has better wine yet to
give me.

God does not call us to be superior to other people; he
calls us to be superior to our previous selves.

*Lord Jesus, I'm thinking of the wedding feast and the
wine. Do it tomorrow for me. Amen.*

Second Fiddle

> He announced to the people, "The man who
> will come after me is much greater than I am."
>
> Mark 1:7 TEV

Week 3, Day 6

Kent works hard at the shoe factory, but he's never made foreman. He sings in the church choir, but never does a solo. On the community softball team he warms the bench.

"I always play second fiddle," he says. "Always the bridesmaid, never the bride. It eats at me so much I can't sleep."

Our position in life keeps us awake. We don't have as much money as our neighbors. The church asks us to do the menial tasks. The boss thinks we do a good job, but we're not executive material. Our club passes over us when it elects officers. We play second fiddle, and we lay awake wishing we didn't.

John the Baptist played second fiddle to Jesus. For a fleeting moment it looked like he might be *the* man; some even whispered he was the Messiah. However, John knew his place in God's plan—not front-runner, but forerunner. John admitted Jesus was the greatest one of the two; he even let his best disciples become disciples of Jesus. He passed from the scene, and Jesus went on to be hailed by millions as the Son of God.

John played second fiddle. But he played it well and I believe he slept well.

I asked our local orchestra leader what second violinists do. He said, "They provide the harmony." Without people in the church, home, factory, office who play second fiddle, there is no harmony in life. Some of us take care of tedious details, do legwork for the up-front leaders, work behind the scenes away from where the spotlight shines brightly on the illustrious stars of the company. But without us, the show couldn't go on.

Second fiddle players please God. He needs all of us to orchestrate his will in the world. When we please God, we should be pleased with ourselves. Being an integral part of God's plan gives self-satisfaction and brings a peace to soothe us as we call it a day.

O God, show me your will and my part in it, your way and my place on it. Amen.

Waiting

"Don't begin telling others yet—stay here in
the city until the Holy Spirit comes and fills
you with power from heaven."

Luke 24:49 TLB

Week 3, Day 7

My son came with a broken toy truck he wanted me to
repair. I said I'd work on it, got the pliers and some glue,
and began the job. In five minutes, Kenneth came back
and asked, "Have you fixed it yet?"

"No, but I'm working on it, son." Another five minutes and he returned. "Daddy, what's taking you so
long?"

We don't wait very well, do we? We lay in bed,
worrying over why things don't happen sooner in our
lives. We wish we'd reach our sales quota right
away. We want our children to mature faster than
they do. And why doesn't God give me more spiritual
power immediately?

My son Kenneth, with his frequent inquiries, only
postponed the toy repair. Finally he left me alone, and
the truck was fixed in a few minutes.

We sleep better when we trust God enough to leave
our "broken toys" with him, when we don't give him a
problem with one hand and impatiently take it back
with the other.

Jesus told the disciples to stay in the city and wait for the Holy Spirit. "Don't call me, I'll call you." But the disciples didn't do that. They got busy, had an election, and chose Matthias to take Judas' place. We never again hear about Matthias because that's not who God had in mind; it was Paul God was thinking of.

The title of Malcolm Boyd's book, *Are You Running With Me, Jesus?* makes this point. We get ahead of God's will and wonder why he doesn't catch up with us. The biblical witness calls us to realize God makes plans which he unveils in his time, not ours. "Wait for the Lord; be strong, and let your heart take courage; yea, wait for the Lord!" (Psalms 27:14). "So you, by the help of your God, return, hold fast to love and justice, and wait continually for your God" (Hosea 12:6).

Dear Lord, I go to sleep now to rest on your promises and wait for your word. Amen.

Whenever

> Between three and six o'clock in the morning Jesus came to the disciples, walking on the water.
>
> Matthew 14:25 TEV

Week 4, Day 1

Twenty percent of the employed population in this country works a night shift. These people have an inverted pattern; they work while most sleep and sleep while most work.

The disciples are out in the lake between three and six o'clock in the morning; perhaps they are fishing to provide food for them and their Master. Jesus desires their company so much he walks on the water to be with them.

Jesus, through the Holy Spirit, comes to us no matter what our schedules. Day *and* night he visits every factory and office building. The same time he is with me as I sleep, he is with others as they work. He desires our company so much he comes to us whenever.

Dazie cleans an office building in Atlanta. She goes there at 11:00 P.M. and works until 7:00 A.M. She labors by herself, with no one in the building except the night security guard. I asked her, "Dazie, don't you get lonely?"

"Never," she replied. "Jesus is there with me; he works all the shifts."

Curious about her sleeping habits, I said, "But don't you have trouble sleeping during the day?"

"No. I figure if Jesus keeps me through the night, he'll help me sleep through the day."

I asked the question because most people who work a night shift have trouble sleeping when they come home. In spite of the increasing numbers of night workers, 20 percent do not make a nocturnal society. During the day there are many distractions: light comes through the windows; people move around in the house; cars go noisily down the street.

Because of these distractions, Zack sleeps only four hours a day. On Saturdays and Sundays he sleeps thirteen hours each night to pay back the "sleep debt." The deprivation during the week leaves him tired and irritable; the catch-up on the weekends robs him of precious time with his family. I put Zack in touch with Dazie, and her testimony worked wonders for him. He's not where she is, but he's on his way.

Dear Jesus, walk with me as I work, and stay with me as I sleep, whenever it is. Amen.

Whatever

So the Lord God caused a deep sleep to fall
upon the man.

Genesis 2:21

Week 4, Day 2

There are three basic types of insomnia. I've suffered
all of them.

1. *Sleep-onset insomnia:* We lie awake for hours re-
viewing the day's events, going over each detail. What
should I have said? What could I have done? Or we
wonder what tomorrow will bring.

Recently I couldn't get to sleep as I worried about the
next day's agenda. I thought of getting up to read a
book, but I lay there thinking any minute I'd doze off.
Finally I did, but not until three hours later.

*Dear Lord, let me feel your comforting presence as I
first go to bed.*

2. *Sleep-maintenance insomnia:* The most common of
all, it affects 50 percent of insomniacs. Sleep is frag-
mented, giving us no profound rest. We ride a shuttle
that takes us endlessly back and forth between the sleep
world and the day world. We relive yesterday and anticipate tomorrow in between naps, get up feeling as if
we've had no sleep at all.

Often my sleep starts, suddenly stops, and starts

again. I toss and turn until I'm exhausted, get a few winks, and wake up again.

Dear Lord, when I wake up in the middle of the night, may I know you are still with me.

3. *Terminal insomnia:* We awake early in the morning long before we have to get up, never hearing the radio alarm because an internal alarm goes off first. I suffer most from this type. In bed, awake at 5:30 A.M., I begin planning my day, needing to get back in the day world and finish what I've left undone or control what I think might happen. Waking too early, by midafternoon I'm worn out.

Dear Lord, when I wake up too early, help me return to the sleep you have for me.

No matter what insomnia we experience, God understands our difficulty, moves to meet us in the midst of it, and does for us what we helplessly attempt to do by ourselves.

O God, I suffer from ————— insomnia. Whenever I need it, cause a deep sleep to fall upon me. Amen.

Inside Out

"But the things which come out of a man are
what defile him."

Mark 7:15

Week 4, Day 3

Robert practices medicine, and his office is packed
every day. Once he said to me, "Many of my patients
need your help more than they need mine."

"What do you mean?" I inquired.

"They can't sleep, but that's not a physical problem;
it's a spiritual one. I give them medication, but that deals
with the symptom, not the source. What they need is a
deep faith and a clear conscience."

Two-thirds of insomniacs go to medical doctors for
help. But medication focuses only on immediate relief.
In fact, most medication becomes ineffective after a
couple of weeks because a tolerance develops.

People not at home in the sleep world are often not at
home in the day world. Sedatives do not cure attitudes
and actions that keep us awake. More than medication
we need meditation. "On his law he meditates day and
night" (Psalms 1:2). The sleep world depends on the day
world. What we hold inside us as faith and trust exter-
nalizes through our sleeping habits.

Merri doesn't sleep well because she can't find her

identity. She lays awake asking over and over again the psychological question, "Who am I?" She hasn't found the right job or the significant relationship because she doesn't know who she is.

I suggested Merri ask the theological question, "Whose am I?" along with the psychological one, then put the two together: "I know who I am when I know whose I am." The persons God made us to be emerge as we affirm the source of our personhood: God the Father, who gives us identity by creating us; God the Son, who enhances that identity with his gift of saving love on the cross; God the Holy Spirit, who empowers us to become who we can be through both creation and salvation. When we know who and whose we are, identity and peace are forged within and we sleep better.

O God, I believe I am yours and you are mine. We are to-gether tonight and in the morning. Amen.

Sharing Troubles

I pour out my complaint before him, I tell my
trouble before him.

Psalms 142:2

Week 4, Day 4

I asked Denise what she does when she can't sleep.

"I make a list of everything that troubled me that day,
put the list on my bed, and kneel in front of it. I say,
'Here it is, Lord; you take care of it. I'm going to sleep.' "

The next morning Denise, rested as God carried her
load through the night, looks at the list in a different
way.

Her troubles seldom seem as serious in the morning
hour. Often she can't imagine why she was anxious at
all. Daylight symbolizes a hope darkness does not.

The list she makes sorts out her troubles, ranks them,
puts them in black and white so they are no longer un-
defined shadows.

When she tells God to take care of her troubles for a
few hours, she celebrates an act of surrender and claims
God's promise.

Mostly, Denise's practice teaches her who God is. He
is the one in front of whom we can be ourselves; we need
wear no masks before him. He listens to our complaints,
looking us in the eye as he does. God never gazes away
as if he has something else on his mind. He waits for us

to finish before he begins speaking; God does not inundate us with advice before he hears us out. He doesn't make fun of us for worrying; he may gently rebuke us with silence or urge us to a more significant concern, but he permits us to pour out our complaints before him.

My friend Ken and I met once a week for two years to pray together. At first my prayers were couched in theological language, wrapped in ambiguity and always qualified, almost into meaninglessness. Ken's prayers never were. He'd say, "O God, I've had an awful day and this is why," or, "Dear Lord, I don't love ————— and I'm not even sure I want to." Ken taught me how to pray: honest and up-front with God.

God hears our complaints and listens to our troubles. He *is* our Father.

My Father in heaven and on earth, carry my load now as I go to sleep; bring the light of your wisdom to my troubles in the morning. Amen.

Praise From Others

Let another praise you, and not your own
mouth.

Proverbs 27:2

Week 4, Day 5

My insatiable need for affirmation keeps me awake. I
go to bed feeling unappreciated and not noticed. I try
bragging on myself, going over the day's events saying,
"I thought that was a good sermon I preached," or, "I
don't know anybody else who could chair that commit-
tee any better than I."

My self-praise rings hollow; I'm not the least bit con-
vincing. Uncertain about my ability, I need someone
else to stroke me.

Others do stroke me, but often I miss it. Thinking I'm
not worth as much as I should be, I don't hear compli-
ments when they come. "They must be talking about
someone else," I say. Or I dismiss the source of praise as
uninformed. "What would they know about it?" Sometimes I receive praise, but I want more. "Sure, they said I
did a good job, but they weren't very enthusiastic about
it."

Several years ago I spent three weeks with Carlyle
Marney, one of the most perceptive people I've known.
After I shared with him my need for affirmation, he

asked, "Phil, the last time you preached, how many people said it was a good sermon?"

"Oh, I don't know, about twenty-five I guess."

Marney replied, "My goodness, how much affirmation do you need?"

If we need excessive affirmation, we should look within ourselves and ask why. Why am I insecure when God has blessed me so much? Doesn't God show his appreciation all the time? Am I missing the affirmation others give me every day?

The affirmation I need is there, a gift from God to me through others. Where I'm realistic, that affirmation satisfies my needs, gives me humility and gratitude.

As I prepare for sleep, I pray, "Dear Lord, open my eyes to the strokes you send through others and close my eyes in thanksgiving and peace."

Holy Spirit, help me receive the special touch of friends and strangers you gave me today. Amen.

Chosen

But you are a chosen race, a royal priesthood,
a holy nation, God's own people.

1 Peter 2:9

Week 4, Day 6

Dean sleeps well in spite of business trips around the
world, lonely hotel rooms, and jet lag. I've discovered
why. Both a successful corporation president and an in-
fluential Christian entrepreneur, he believes God
chooses him for unique and important tasks. Dean feels
called to do what he does best: practice Jesus' love as he
relates to his employees and sponsor Christian ministries
of evangelism.

When we feel God's call to specific tasks, two dynamics occur. First, we believe God knows who we are and
what we can do. Receiving God's confidence in us, we
feel positive about ourselves. Second, we believe if God
calls us, he will equip us. We feel God's presence in our
undertakings.

Self-confidence and awareness of divine presence fur-
nish the dynamics that create calmness and bring restful
sleep.

Knowing we are selected and enlisted by God for his
work provides the clearest path to peace. We throw open
the windows and declare, "I know this one great thing;

I'm wanted for the business of the King." A path of daytime purpose paves the road to nighttime sleep.

Marlene proves this premise. She had difficulty sleeping until God called her to minister to the deaf. In her church, she "signs" worship services and teaches a Sunday school class for the deaf. Before, she felt out of touch with her life's purpose, but now she's convinced God has ordained and enabled her. Her insomnia first decreased and then disappeared.

We rest on God's serene pillows when we find and fulfill God's unique purpose for us.

O God, show me my path of purpose and help me walk in it. Amen.

Intercession for Us

I do not cease to give thanks for you, remembering you in my prayers.

Ephesians 1:16

Week 4, Day 7

Frequently, as I prepare for sleep, I remember all the people who pray for me. I know Mom never fails to include me in her prayers. Dick and Betty promise to lift me up to God, and they do. A prayer group in Atlanta has me on its list. A church in a nearby town intercedes for my ministry every Sunday. My wife keeps my name on her prayerful lips, and my children remember Dad when they talk with God.

Assured of this intercession, I sleep better, just as I think the Ephesian congregation did after they read Paul's letter. With such a faithful saint as Paul praying for them, they must have been more at peace as they turned in for the night.

Carol came to the church prayer group troubled and upset. Some would have stayed home because of trauma, but Carol came because of it. She said, "I'm so glad it's Tuesday night, so my friends can pray for me." We did, and she went home believing God would help her through the night and bring a better day.

To find comfort through intercessory prayer we must:

1. Build a network of interceders, ask people of prayer to remember us, fill out prayer request cards when we visit a new church, form groups where we pray for each other.

2. Believe prayers are heard and answered, trust God's response to Christians praying for each other, know "the heartfelt supplication of a righteous man" exerts a mighty influence (James 5:16 WEYMOUTH).

3. Pray for those who pray for us, join the community of intercession. As we call each name, praying for others, we feel their prayers for us.

Dear God, thank you for all those who pray for me to-night. Amen.

Past Triumphs

> And why need I say more? For time will fail
> me if I tell the story of Gideon, Barak, Sam-
> son, Jephthah, and of David and Samuel and
> the Prophets; men who, through faith, con-
> quered whole kingdoms.
> Hebrews 11:32, 33 WEYMOUTH

Week 5, Day 1

The author of Hebrews needs assurance, so he takes a trip back through history, remembering those whose faith God rewarded with triumph.

The past often keeps us awake, but it can also lull us to sleep. We rest better when we claim the victories God has already given.

Victories he's given to our predecessors: the founding fathers of our country who started what we now cherish; the faithful people who built the churches in which we worship; the community leaders whose foresight pro-vides a comfort that is ours to enjoy; our parents who did whatever was necessary to give us significant oppor-tunities.

We sleep well when we remember the victories in our own lives: the education we got; the mate God gave us, without whom we'd be incomplete; the spiritual di-rection we received when the street we walked seemed a dead end, the job that blesses us with the money we need.

The time before sleep can be eucharistic when we thank God for what he has done. Praising God for the past leaves little room for second-guessing and regret, both of which postpone sleep.

A hospital in which I was a patient had a crucifix on the wall facing the bed. Each night I thought of Jesus who died for me. Without wine and bread I still remembered the sacrificial love and redeeming grace of the cross. Each night as I prepared for sleep, I experienced Eucharist. What a thought to go to bed on!

Lord Jesus, I remember you. Remember me as I sleep. Amen.

Bedroom Altar

Then Noah built an altar to the Lord.
                              Genesis 8:20

Week 5, Day 2

Nicole uses her nightstand as an altar. She places there a wooden cross her fifth-grade Sunday-school class made for her, two candles in glass holders she bought for a dollar each, and a picture of Jesus she cut out of a magazine and framed. Each night she kneels and prays in front of her altar.

Leah uses her sewing machine as an altar. Before going to bed, she clears away the thread, needles, and material scraps, an exercise she says symbolizes shutting out the day's demands. The clearing away prepares her for worship and over the months has become worship itself. Leah puts on the sewing machine table a bronze cross and candlestick her father gave her twenty-five years ago as a confirmation gift and places her Bible in front of the cross. She reads a verse or two to call her to prayer. Leah can't kneel because of an automobile accident, so she sits in a chair, lights the candles, thanks God for today, and claims his presence for tomorrow.

Our bedrooms provide appropriate places to worship God too. The day over, the children asleep, the house quiet, we can experience a solitude rich in meditation as we prepare for sleep.

Josh and Martha worship together propped up in bed on soft pillows. They both bring a symbol of their praise and lay it on their laps. Josh often brings a horn of plenty from the kitchen to signify his blessings, Martha a wooden cross necklace or a picture one of their children has drawn. Once Josh brought a saw he'd used to build a new room onto their house. With the symbols in place, Josh and Martha give their testimonies of praise, indicating the gratitude each item represents. They pray together and sing the Doxology. Then they go to sleep.

O God, make my bedroom a sanctuary in which I bless your holy name. Amen.

What We Have

But Peter said, "I have no silver and gold, but I give you what I have."

Acts 3:6

Week 5, Day 3

Mason is a bighearted man who wants to help everyone. When he does a good deed he says, "I wish I could do more." In his estimation, he never does enough and he lies awake at night regretting his inadequacy. But Mason never fails me. He always does more for me than I expect and never less than I need. However, I can't convince him of that.

Peter faces a congenital cripple who begs for money. Peter has no money, so it seems he can't meet the cripple's needs. However, Peter focuses on realities, not fantasies. He takes no trips to the world of what might be, but lives in the realm of what is. He gives the cripple what he has, and the man walks away healed and whole.

Often we hold back our abilities with excuses of incompetence. "I'm not up to that." "So much to do and I have so little to do it with." We deny the good in us, which is as dishonest as denying the bad. God asks us only for what he's given us.

Holding back gives Stan a cop-out. Because he can't do everything, he does nothing. He wakes up before he should, lamenting his inaction and feeling guilty because he withholds what he has.

When we accept the abilities we have and use them to glorify God, we go to bed satisfied enough to sleep. We turn in for the night on the note of praise, thanking God for his gifts. Thanking God, we acknowledge him as Lord. We call it a day, feeling good about ourselves; we did what we could, and God blessed it beyond our dreams. Self-satisfaction gives us the peace to sleep. We rest well, preparing ourselves for tomorrow when we again can honor God by using what we have to fulfill his will.

O God, I affirm my gifts and promise I'll use them tomorrow for you. Amen.

Always Light

> If I say, "Let only darkness cover me, and the
> light about me be night," even the darkness is
> not dark to thee, the night is bright as the day;
> for darkness is as light with thee."
>
> Psalms 139:11

Week 5, Day 4

Timmy takes two hours every night to get to sleep. His
mother puts him to bed, but five minutes later he's up
wanting a glass of water. In the winter Timmy says he's
too cold to sleep; in the summer he's too hot. Once he
got up complaining of "lumpy things" in the bed.
Timmy's big sister, a child psychologist, came to visit
and discovered his problem. He's afraid of the dark.

Darkness fear also affects many adults, particularly
older people who associate darkness with death and stay
awake, fearing they'll die if they close their eyes. Darkness disturbs some adults so much they sleep with the
light on.

Madge, forty-two years old, painted her room the
brightest yellow she could find, leaves her bed lamp on,
and has night-lights plugged in at every receptacle. She
even arranged her work schedule so she could come
home early and sleep in the afternoon.

Darkness seems hopeless and final. We associate it
with defeat and even death. But darkness provides an

essential ingredient in God's plan for us. It shuts out the day world, changes the pace, and honors the biological rhythm within us. Darkness pulls the shades down over a busy day. We no longer have to "smell the smoke" of hectic activity in our nostrils. It asks us to cooperate with God's balance; we rest to work, retreat to advance. Darkness brings a trust in God; we believe he'll keep the light of his love around us even in the night. We depend on God, who said, "Let light shine out of darkness" (2 Corinthians 4:6).

He still says it. He still does it.

Dear Lord, I lay here in the dark, knowing your light surrounds me. Amen.

Family Altars

All these with one accord devoted themselves
to prayer, together with the women and Mary
the mother of Jesus, and with his brothers.

Acts 1:14

Week 5, Day 5

We've heard it said, "The family that prays together stays together." Also, the family that prays together sleeps well. Family altars produce qualities conducive to sound sleep.

They bring harmony. When all family members join in praying for one another, relationships improve and loyalty develops. Going to bed pleased about family love puts a soothing song in our souls.

Family altars clear the air. Combined with moments of sharing, they give everyone a chance to be honest, to tell what's happening to them and feel good that they can.

A praying family identifies needs. Something we didn't know about a child, a sister, even a parent, surfaces, and we know better where to focus our love.

When we pray together, we ask God to help us with our families. We say he can do more with our relationships than we can do by ourselves. God becomes the orientation of everyone and accompanies us to our bedrooms.

How do we initiate a family altar?

The Parkers bring everyone into Mom and Dad's bedroom. The teenage twins sit on the floor, and little Bobby crawls in bed with his parents. Dad reads a psalm, and Mom tells what it means to her. One of the twins prays for each family member by name, and Bobby gets to say "Amen" at the end of the prayer.

The Wilsons meet around the kitchen table as soon as everyone is in the house. They use the church's devotional book, taking turns each night reading different parts. One reads the Scripture, another the memory verse, one the message, another the prayer.

The methodology comes if the desire is deep and the intention real. We do what we need and want to do. We need time together as a family loving each other and praising God. We want to give God a chance to make his presence felt.

O God, gather up my family in your arms tonight and help me show your love to each one. Amen.

Music Soothes

I will sing of thy steadfast love, O Lord, for
ever.

Psalms 89:1

Week 5, Day 6

Many people turn on a good soft FM station at night.
They believe "music soothes the savage breast" and cre-
ates an atmosphere for sleep.

I often listen to classical music in bed. Beethoven's
Sixth Symphony mellows my soul; even its name, the
Pastoral, settles my restlessness. Debussy's *Iberia,* par-
ticularly the second movement, "The Fragrance of
Night," brings serenity to me.

Recently I found a religious radio station that plays
hymns in full orchestra. No vocal; just soft strings pouring out music I associate with comfort, assurance, and
peace. As I listen to "Amazing Grace" and "Standing on
the Promises," I receive the blessing of God's presence
and fall asleep in his strong arms.

Such music gives form to our inner feelings and de-
taches us from the day's difficulties. It transports our
feelings to God, and he accepts them and loves us as we
share our inner spaces with him. Robert Browning said,
"Who hears music, feels his solitude peopled at once."

Music conducive to sleep must be chosen wisely.
Some modern music sounds as if it had not been com-

posed but decomposed. It cannot soothe the savage breast when it's savage itself.

Abbie selects gospel music associated with her conversion experience. Through the songs, she relives the beginning of her relationship with Jesus and affirms the joy of the Lord's love as she goes to bed. Kahlil Gibran said, "Music is an extension of hearing." Abbie hears God's quieting word in the songs of faith.

"Let the word of Christ dwell in you richly . . . as you sing psalms and hymns and spiritual songs with thankfulness in your hearts to God" (Colossians 3:16).

O God, I go to bed with the music of your love in my soul. Amen.

Daily Bread

> Then the Lord said to Moses, "Behold, I will
> rain bread from heaven for you; and the peo-
> ple shall go out and gather a day's portion
> every day, that I may prove them, whether
> they walk in my law or not."
>
> Exodus 16:4

Week 5, Day 7

Nat says, "My portfolio includes life-insurance poli-
cies to benefit my family if I die young, major medical
protection in case someone has a sustained illness, and a
savings account for a rainy day. I stock my freezer with
two months supply of food, and the well-filled cupboard
could take us through a considerable famine. Still, the
thought deters my sleep: Do I have enough?"

But Eric and Faye live austerely, giving others more
than they presently need. Eric's suits go to Goodwill before they're out of style. "I only need two," he says. Faye
gives furniture away because "we have more than we
can all sit on at one time."

Of course God wants us to plan wisely for tomorrow,
take care of our families, and provide for the future. But
he doesn't want us to obsess ourselves with more and
better, forgetting he takes care of us daily.

God told Israel to gather enough manna for each day.

Israel disobeyed and gathered more than a day's supply; the manna bred worms and became foul.

Bridgette's freezer was filled with three sides of beef, bushels of vegetables, and ten pies she'd baked and frozen. One day the electric power failed and everything in the freezer spoiled. "I live too far in advance," she said.

Abner put several thousand dollars in the stock market; the market plummeted and he couldn't even recover his investment. "I should have spent that money for what we need now," he lamented.

When we hoard things, we live in the future and miss the present. Anyway, we don't know what the future holds, so how can we possibly determine when we have enough stored away?

God told Moses the reason for the one-day policy: "that I may prove them, whether they walk in my law or not." God wants us to trust him enough to live one day at a time. He takes care of the birds of the air and the lilies of the field, he'll take care of us as well.

O Lord, give me my daily bread tomorrow. Amen.

Immediate Help

Then Peter climbed down from the boat and
walked upon the water to go to Him. But when
he felt the wind he grew frightened, and beginning to sink he cried out, "Master, save
me."

               Matthew 14:29, 30 WEYMOUTH

Week 6, Day 1

Derald's architectural business suffered hard times.
New construction nearly stopped, and clients had no
money to pay him for work already completed. One
night Derald couldn't get to sleep, a new experience for
him. At 4:00 A.M. he jumped out of bed, got on his
knees, and prayed, "Lord, help me get to sleep right
now!" Sharing this experience at our prayer meeting,
Derald said, "You know what? He did. I got back in bed
and went to sleep immediately."

That doesn't work for everyone and provides no
magic formula. It worked for Derald because he was
desperate, audacious, trusting, and cooperative.

Staying awake, anticipating we'll be worn out tomorrow, makes us desperate. If we don't get to sleep soon,
we don't know what we'll do. God hears our anxiety and
lets us lean on him when all else has failed.

If we're audacious enough to cry out to him. A sleepless

night is no time for timidity or false humility. Jesus told us we receive when we ask.

If we're trusting enough to believe God can help us. I lay awake one night and finally prayed, "O God, if you can set the stars in place, I know you can help me get to sleep."

Desperation, audacity, trust, and, next, cooperation. We must believe God does his part, then do ours. Rejoice and relax. Breathe out anxiety; breathe in tranquility. Feel yourself go limp in God's arms.

Dear Jesus, what I seek I find. I knock and the door to sleep opens. Amen.

What We Eat

So, whether you eat or drink, or whatever you
do, do all to the glory of God.
                              1 Corinthians 10:31

Week 6, Day 2

Danny discovered the reason for his sleeplessness; he
calls it "the bologna syndrome." Every night he makes a
"Dagwood sandwich": bread, mustard, mayonnaise, let-
tuce, tomato, and piles of bologna. He eats the sandwich
just before going to bed. The normal time for getting to
sleep is fifteen minutes, but Danny takes two hours.
Consulting his doctor, he learned we need at least two
hours between eating and sleeping for the stomach to
complete its digestive task.

However, some foods contain the chemical L-trytophan, which facilitates sleep. The best source is turkey,
which may explain why we fall asleep after Thanksgiving dinner. It's also found in other protein-rich foods
such as cheese, eggs, and milk. The advice "Drink a
glass of milk before bed" is good counsel. Biologically it
provides L-trytophan, and psychologically it revives
childhood memories of security.

Theologically, we glorify God when we watch what
we eat at night. We cooperate with him; God wants us to
rest and be ready for a new day. We honor the bodies he

gives us; we don't abuse his creation. We use the good sense God bestows on us; we aren't stupid about our eating habits.

Tess didn't sleep well until she realized her eating habits can diminish her spiritual life. The unnecessary weight she gains through late-night snacks affects her health; she knows God wants her body sound. Fitful sleep robs her of energy she needs to serve the Lord each day. Tess is changing her eating habits to glorify God.

External control begins with internal commitment. Obedience elicits discipline. We get a handle on our habits when we submit our wills to God's purpose for us.

Dear God, may whatever I do bring honor and glory to your holy name. Amen.

What We Read

You shall read the words of the Lord.
Jeremiah 36:6

Week 6, Day 3

I read myself to sleep almost every night. After fifteen to thirty minutes, my eyes get heavy and I'm ready to call it a day.

I carefully choose what I read. Agatha Christie gets me hooked, and I stay awake to solve the mystery. I never tackle Robert Ludlum's intrigue books late at night.

The Bible serves us well at night, particularly the psalms with their praise and petition. Jesus' miracles are good to read. In them we focus on his power and strength, qualities he uses to keep us safely through the night. Some of Paul's writings, such as Romans 8, remind us of God's love and ability; we sleep better when we rest on divine promises.

Wyatt often reads Philippians 4, lingering a while on verse 19: "And my God will supply every need of yours according to his riches in glory in Christ Jesus." Bill says he reads the saints, "the believers, the trusters in God." He suggests Thomas a Kempis, Henry Drummond, and E. Stanley Jones.

Reading in bed becomes a tranquillizer we can depend on. It symbolizes the end of a day and builds a bridge between the day world and the sleep world. It deprograms us from a hectic routine. Reading the right things banishes day-world thoughts and puts in our minds God's thoughts. We trust God to lead us through a period of decompression and direct us to the peaceful night he intends us to have.

O God, I read your words, know your presence, and trust your strength. Amen.

Getting Comfortable

Taking one of the stones of the place, he put it
under his head and lay down in that place to
sleep.

Genesis 28:11

Week 6, Day 4

Our daughter went to summer camp with the usual
gear plus her personal pillow. The camp furnished pillows but Lisa said, "I can't sleep on one of theirs; I have
to have mine."

Many of us need particular physical conditions so we
can sleep. Unlike Jacob, "any old rock" won't do.

Our bodies must be assured of comfort before they
respond to the mind's desire to sleep. We need a proper
amount of warmth or the coolness keeps us overstimu-
lated. Too much warmth makes us break out in a sweat
and we feel suffocated.

The pillow plays a large role; big ones provide security for some but overwhelm others. Reggie likes a hard
pillow because it keeps his head directly horizontal to
the rest of his body. Michael prefers a pliable pillow, so
his head feels surrounded by softness.

Some people shop endlessly until they find the right
mattress. Parker bought the firmest one he could find
and then put a board under it. "I want no sinking sensa-

tion," he says. Albert likes a mattress he can get lost in. "I feel secure when I'm enveloped."

I can't sleep when it's hot, but I'm allergic to air-conditioning. After twenty-one years in Georgia, I now live in a cooler climate. With the windows open and the fresh air pouring in, I rest better.

Whatever our needs, God wants us to recognize and meet them. He gives us pillows, mattresses, different degrees of temperature; we honor him when we determine the right gift for us and use it. God provides; we are partners with him when we utilize discernment and good sense. What a great God who's concerned about such things!

O God, thank you for loving me enough to give me what I need. Amen.

Sleep Positions

> And a young man named Eutychus was sitting
> in the window. He sank into a deep sleep as
> Paul talked still longer; and being overcome by
> sleep, he fell down from the third story and
> was taken up for dead.
>
> Acts 20:9

Week 6, Day 5

Eutychus chose a poor sleep position: sitting up.

The position in which we sleep is important. Four are
most common. *The semi-fetal:* We curl up in a womblike
posture, but not completely. More people sleep this way
than any other. It brings a sense of security we need and
don't feel in the day world, or it symbolizes a stability
we already have. *The full-fetal:* Curled up, head and
knees touching, we seek the protection of prebirth or act
out the impregnable nature that is ours every day. *Prone:*
On our stomach, stretched out, taking over the bed, we
indicate either the desire or the ability to control our
lives. *Royal:* On our backs, sometimes our hands under
our heads, we demonstrate self-confidence or the search
for it.

Sleep positions frequently reveal stress. Aware of this,
we learn our reactions to the day world. We can study
nightly symptoms to better understand daily pressures.
Roscoe sleeps with one foot hanging out of the bed,

touching the floor. He learned this often means a person can't let go of something in his life. Roscoe couldn't forget his job responsibilities even when he slept. Cognizant of his tension, he asks God each night to deliver him from it.

We sleep better when we determine what our positions symbolize and choose the one best for us. Lloyd needs more security than his royal position allows, so he switched to the semi-fetal. Pete slept prone for years, but when his wife died, that position didn't work and he changed to the full-fetal. Connie experienced a healing miracle in her life and moved from full-fetal to royal.

Whatever position we take in bed, God is there with us to see us through the night, rested and ready for a new day.

Dear Lord, thank you for understanding who I am and being who you are. Amen.

No Fear

In love there can be no fear, but fear is driven
out by perfect love.

1 John 4:18 JERUSALEM

Week 6, Day 6

Lloyd's of London makes millions of dollars betting
that what people fear won't happen.

Many of us don't sleep well because of fear. We're
afraid of the dark, horrified about tomorrow's possibili-
ties, alarmed over today's consequences. Some fear we
won't wake up if we go to sleep.

Most of what we fear never happens. It's like facing a
firing squad; we look into the gun barrels, and our hearts
clench inside us. They can't miss at that range; the end is
near. But when the signal to fire is given, the guns click
emptily. They weren't loaded at all. Most fears are between our ears.

Still, fear keeps us awake. How do we deal with this
disturber of our sleep?

We take on a greater quality. We send love to answer
the door when fear knocks.

When I'm afraid enough to stay awake, I look at my
wife, Sharon, sound asleep beside me. I think how much
I love her and how much she loves me. With that kind
and degree of love, can anything at all frighten me?

Steve gets out of bed, goes to his four-year-old's room, watches her carefree sleep, and remembers her hug when he came home from work. "My apprehensions have no credibility when I look at Jenny."

Mary erected a plaque on her bedroom wall and reads it when fear comes. It says, "God loves you as if you're the only one."

God loves us with a perfect, unconditional, unreserved love. I know he loves everyone that way, but there's so much for me it seems I'm the only one. Feasting on God's love, we have no time or need to eat at the table of fear.

O God, what have I to fear when you love me so much.
Amen.

Grace First

Grace and peace to you in fullest measure.
1 Peter 1:2 NEB

Week 6, Day 7

I like Peter's sequence: grace first and then peace. Paul does the same thing in Ephesians 1:2, "Grace to you and peace from God our Father and the Lord Jesus Christ."

Sometimes we put the cart before the horse. We seek peace to comfort our anxieties and get us to sleep without considering the grace we already have. Peace is a consequence of grace, a reward when we receive God's love for us. Grace is the unmerited act of God's love to win us to him; the result of such favor is peace.

We don't deserve grace, but we get it anyway. It's like the shining of the sun. Does the sun shine because the flowers deserve its warmth? Because the earth earns its rays? No. The sun shines because it is the sun's nature to do so. God's grace comes to us because of his nature.

Thomas Harris writes in *I'm OK—You're OK,* "The central message of Christ's ministry was the concept of grace. Grace is a 'loaded' word, but it's difficult to find one to replace it. The concept of grace ... is a theological way of saying, 'I'm OK—you're OK.' It is not you can be OK, if; or you will be accepted, if; but rather YOU ARE ACCEPTED, unconditionally."

Often I stay awake because I believe I'm not okay, or I fear others think little of me. Grace comes to me in the middle of the night and tells me I am okay because God says so.

Grace is the channel through which God's spiritual blessings flow to us, faith the means by which we receive them, peace the consequence of God's action and our response.

Shelley takes a page from Martin Luther; when she can't sleep she says over and over, "I've been baptized and blessed in Jesus Christ." She acknowledges grace, gains peace, and goes to sleep.

O Lord Jesus, thank you for grace I don't deserve, but get anyway. Amen.

Thirty Ways to Help Us Sleep

1. Change what we can. Delete late-night television or disturbing novels.
2. Think pleasant thoughts. Create positive and peaceful images.
3. Prepare through prayer. Commend ourselves to God as the day's final act.
4. Include others. Share the day's last minutes with our loved ones.
5. Set things straight. Reconcile any hurt or oversight.
6. Watch our diets. Don't stuff ourselves with midnight snacks we can't digest.
7. Expect God's presence. Anticipate that God will stay in the bedroom with us through the night.

8. Get some exercise. Do something physical to get our bodies ready for sleep.

9. Get comfortable. Check the thermostat, the bed covers, the windows.

10. Stroke ourselves. Think of the good we accomplished today.

11. Focus on friends. Consider those who love us and pray for us.

12. Affirm our faith. Acknowledge we belong to God.

13. Read the Bible. Center on the great passages of petition.

14. Consider others. Intercede for people who need assurance of God's love.

15. Anticipate tomorrow. Rest in order to be fresh and alert.

16. Don't dread dreams. Receive dreams as part of God's revelation.

17. Use a technique. Try breathing exercises or body manipulation.

18. Encourage mysticism. Feel Jesus' presence until we see him.

19. Celebrate interruptions. Enjoy the surprises God sent today.

20. Claim serendipity. Look forward to the surprises God sends tomorrow.

21. Accept ourselves. What we do is important.

22. Anticipate growth. Tomorrow will be better than today.

23. Don't rush things. Wait on God to bless us in his time.

24. Be honest. Admit what keeps us awake and seek God's help.
25. Make a separation. Divide the day world from the sleep world.
26. Build a bridge. Ease ourselves from the day world into the sleep world.
27. Affirm our election. Know God chooses us for particular purposes.
28. Commune with Nature. Find a place where we see God's handiwork.
29. Don't be afraid. God never takes a vacation.
30. Worship last. Go to bed on the note of praise.